Great Names in Sports

Coordinating Editor
MORTON BOTEL, ED.D.
*Associate Professor of Education,
Graduate School of Education, University of Pennsylvania*
*Formerly Assistant Superintendent in Curriculum and Research,
Bucks County, Pennsylvania, School System*

Great Names in Sports

by Martin Buskin
and Howard Hagler

Illustrated by Jack Breslow

Follett Publishing Company   *Chicago*

Library of Congress Catalog Card Number: 68-14102

To Saundra and Micky

CAN YOU READ THIS BOOK?

Before you start reading *Great Names in Sports,* read the words in this table to someone. Count the words you can read.

caught	newspaper
change	only
even	picked
face	quickly
grass	quiet
kept	really
later	than
learned	wind
leg	world
most	year

How many words could you read? That will tell you how well you can read this book.

10–13 words	This book may be too hard for you.
14–16 words	You can read this book with help on some words.
17–18 words	This book will be easy for you.
19–20 words	This book may be very easy for you.

BOTH HANDS FOR JESSE

Jesse Owens was so good that people couldn't believe he was real. At 21, he set three world's records. No one had ever done so well at both running and jumping.

The next year Jesse was picked for the United States Olympic team. It was 1936. The games were being held in Berlin, Germany.

9

Adolf Hitler, the leader of Germany, said Jesse could not win. Hitler was sure an American couldn't win. And he was sure a Negro couldn't win. Jesse was both.

It was the third day of the games. Jesse and a German, Lutz Long, were in the broad jump. Jesse wanted very much to win. He wanted to show that he *could* do it.

Each man would get three tries. Jesse got set to jump. But first he ran a little way down the track. They said he had used up one of his jumps by running!

Jesse was mad. But he tried not to be. He knew he wouldn't be any good if he was mad. He started out again down the short track.

But this time they said that his foot went over the line as he started to jump! He was supposed to jump from behind the line. Again they said he had made a bad jump. Jesse had just one try left.

This time he made it. But Lutz Long made it too. He jumped just as far as Jesse did. So they both had to jump again.

On this jump, Jesse felt like he was flying. The people let out a long OOOOH!

When Jesse came down, he just knew it was a great jump. He was right. Jesse had set a new Olympic record—more than 26 feet!

The people all got up and shouted for him. Lutz
Long told him he was the greatest of them all.

But Hitler, the leader of Germany, wouldn't talk to
Jesse or shake his hand. He had been sure that a German would win. So he only shook Lutz Long's hand.

Many years later, in 1951, Jesse Owens went back to Germany. In Berlin, he stood before 75,000 people in the same place where he had set his Olympic record.

Jesse gave a short talk. Then the mayor of Berlin told him, "Fifteen years ago Hitler would not shake your hand. Here, I give you both of mine."

MANTLE UP

They had played two innings when the Dodger pitcher went bad. Now the game was tied, 1-1. The bases were loaded, with two out. And Mickey Mantle was up for the Yankees.

It was 1953. The Yankees had a one-game lead in the World Series. The Dodgers had won two games, and the Yankees had won three. If the Yankees took this game they would win the Series.

The Dodger manager called for time. Mickey moved around. He saw the manager walk out to talk to the pitcher. Roy Campanella, the big Dodger catcher, went out there too.

The three men stood together, talking. It seemed like a long time to Mickey.

The manager came off the field with the pitcher behind him. Russ Meyer, a new pitcher, came out and started warming up.

Mickey stepped nearer the batter's box. He looked up at the stands.

He had stood at this spot in Yankee Stadium many times. He thought about the times his hits had helped the team win. He had hit 43 home runs that year.

But he also thought about the times he had struck out. He couldn't strike out now. This game was too big. He just couldn't strike out now!

The runners were moving around, leading off their bases. They were ready to go.

Mickey stepped into the batter's box again and got set for the pitch. Russ Meyer looked down at Campanella a long time before he took the sign.

As Meyer's right arm went back, up, and around, the stands grew very quiet.

It was a fast, low ball. Mickey brought his bat up and around. CRACK! The ball met wood, hard.

As the ball sailed high and far, the people all jumped up and shouted. "Home run! It's gone! A HOMER!" Once again Mickey had gotten the big hit. The Yankees went on to win the Series.

Only three men had ever hit grand-slam homers in a World Series. That day Mickey Mantle had made it four.

THE SIX-DOLLAR QUARTERBACK

That year Pittsburgh had three great quarterbacks, They didn't really need another quarterback—and Johnny Unitas made four.

Pittsburgh had picked him up at a bad time. Johnny just wished he had finished school a year sooner or a year later.

He worked hard on his game. He tried every trick he had learned playing football in school. He held the ball as long as he could before he threw a pass. He wasn't afraid to run when he had to.

But he wasn't as big as some of the other players. And he couldn't seem to show them that he was just as good.

Just before the football year started, the manager told him the team couldn't use him. Johnny would never play in a real game for Pittsburgh.

Now it was so late in the year that he couldn't try out for another team. There was nothing he could do about it. He went back to his hometown, Philadelphia.

Johnny had a family to feed. So he went to work as a builder. But his wife knew he couldn't be happy unless he played football. She wouldn't let him forget what he really wanted.

So Johnny started playing football on Sundays with a hometown team called the Bloomfield Rams. Each man got six dollars a game.

The Rams played their games on a school playground. Only some old people and little boys came to see their games. But Johnny didn't care where they played or how many people came. He was playing football again, and that was all he wanted.

When he played football, Johnny was a new man. He didn't move the same. Even his face didn't look the same. He was happy, all the way.

Now he really started learning football. He started making up the tricks the newspapers later wrote about.

The biggest thing he learned was how to change the play at the line.

One Sunday the two teams were in place, ready to play. Then Johnny looked over the men on the other team. He saw that they were in just the right spots to stop his play.

So he didn't try that play. He called the signal for *another* play, just before the ball was sent back to him. It worked; it was beautiful.

Johnny kept changing the play at the line each time after that. The Rams won just about every game!

Johnny still wasn't paid any more than the other men. He still got six dollars for each game. But he and his wife didn't care about the money. They were two happy people when Johnny was playing football.

One day Johnny got a call from the manager of the Baltimore Colts. He had heard about Johnny and wanted him to try out for the team.

Johnny went to Baltimore as soon as he could. He made the team. And this time he *stayed* on the team.

Johnny Unitas took over, with fire no one knew he had in him. The Colts won game after game.

Football was Johnny's life. In 1957 he was named the most valuable player in the country. And on TV people all over could see what a really happy man looked like!

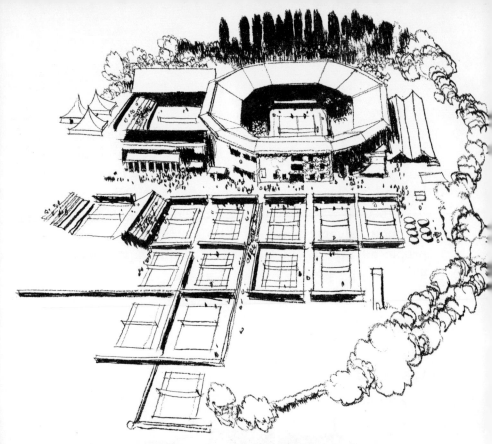

HOT DAY AT WIMBLEDON

It was hot, very hot, that day at Wimbledon, England. But the Queen of England was there. And Althea Gibson was there.

Althea came from New York City.

It had taken her many years to become a great tennis player. She had played at Wimbledon before and lost. Now her thoughts showed on her face: "It's my time to *win*!"

For Wimbledon was more than just a beautiful place to play tennis. This was as far as a tennis player could go. Players who won here showed the world that they were the best.

Newspapermen from all over the world sat in the stands. Today they might see a Negro girl win at Wimbledon. She would be playing Darlene Hard, one of the best. They knew it would be a hot game.

The sun burned down as Althea hit the first ball to Darlene. It was 96° that day!

But Althea said later that she thought the hot sun *helped* her game. "I felt all along that it was my day." The sun only made her feel good.

Althea ran all over her side of the court, making shots no one thought she could.

When Darlene was in close, Althea would drive the ball way back. When Darlene was at the back of the court, Althea would drop the ball in close.

As the game went on, the sun started getting to the people in the stands—and to Darlene.

But Althea played better and better. Some people said she made Darlene look like a beginner. In less than an hour, Althea had won.

"At last! At last!" she kept saying. At last, that day in 1957, Althea Gibson had made it at Wimbledon.

And that wasn't all. She saw the Queen of England step out of her box and walk towards her. Althea went over and took the gold tray the Queen handed her.

Althea thought this was the greatest thing that would ever happen to her.

But that still wasn't all. The next day she got a letter. It said that the people of the United States were proud of her. I thanked her for doing her very best and doing it so well. The letter was signed:

> *With best wishes,*
> *Dwight D. Eisenhower*
> *President of the United States*

WHEN WILLIE STOPPED TRYING

The Giants had lost 11 straight games. They were a good team, but they just didn't pull together. They had no fire.

Then Leo Durocher heard about a boy who was burning up the small town teams. "Just what we need," he thought.

But Willie Mays didn't help much. In his first game for the Giants, he didn't get a hit. He didn't get one in the next game, or the next. In 25 times at bat, he didn't get a hit!

And he was running all over the outfield. He was in all the wrong places at all the wrong times.

In one game he even asked Leo Durocher to take him out. "Mr. Leo," he said, "send me back down. I told you I couldn't hit this pitching."

But Leo said no. He didn't see a bad ballplayer, just a quiet, good-looking boy who was trying too hard.

So he changed Willie's spot. Willie had been batting third. Now Leo had him bat later, so he wouldn't try as hard.

It helped. In the new spot, Willie got better. And the strange thing was that the Giants got better too.

Willie was having such a good time playing ball that the rest of the team picked up his smile. Each

game, the Giants played better and better. They were playing together now.

It was August, 1951. The Giants were way behind the Dodgers. But their big games with the Dodgers were just coming up. And this first game would tell.

It was the 8th inning. The game was tied 1-1. The Dodgers had a man on third, with one man out.

Willie was playing in left center field. But the hit was a fly ball to right center!

Willie started out after it. It wasn't too short a ball or too far out for a good throw.

But it was to his left, away from his throwing arm. After he caught it, he would have to stop and get set before he threw. And that would give the man on third the time he needed to get home.

Willie knew he would have to make the fastest throw of his life. He took another quick look at the ball to guess where it would land. He had an idea. It was a strange idea, but it just might work.

As he caught the ball, he let it help turn him all the way around! By catching and turning at the same time, he could throw faster and harder. He just might catch the runner.

Willie let fly. But the man standing right in line with home plate was too surprised to catch the throw. He just got out of the way!

The ball went sailing on through to home. There the catcher caught it and tagged the runner. And that was that.

No one had ever seen a play like Willie's before. They called it "The Throw." It took the fire right out of the Dodgers.

But it put fire back into the Giants. Now Leo really knew how lucky he was that Willie had stopped trying too hard!

TIME AND ROGER BANNISTER

"Nobody could have wanted to run more than I did."

Roger Bannister wanted to run the mile faster than anyone ever had. It was all he wanted.

He didn't care about winning races. And he didn't care about getting his name in the newspapers. He just wanted to run that fast mile.

Roger was trying to become a doctor. He needed more time to read school books. He needed more time to sleep. But most of all, he wanted more time to run. He knew he had to run four hours or more every day.

Somehow, he found the time to run. His legs got stronger and stronger. At last he knew he was ready.

A light rain was falling that day in spring, 1954. Roger had asked two other runners to race with him. He knew they would make him run faster. The rain might slow him down; but it was too late now to call the race off.

The three men got ready at the starting line. A shot sounded, starting the race. The other two men jumped out in front.

Roger ran slowly at first—once around slowly, then once more. On the third time around, he began to think about his time. As his legs moved up and down, he knew time was moving with them.

Now his legs started to hurt. Now other parts of him were telling him this was too fast, too far. But he didn't listen. He kept running harder, trying not to think.

A shot! It was the sign that he had gone around three times. This would make four—his last time around. He had to do it *now*.

As he rounded the first turn, someone held up a sign. It showed him the time he had made so far. He knew he had to run much faster.

Roger heard his feet. And he could hear time moving, as fast as his feet moved. But he kept running.

Now he couldn't hear anything. He could see men standing around waiting for him at the finish line. He ran to it and over it. Then he fell.

But as he fell, Roger Bannister knew somehow that he had done it. He knew he was the first man to run a mile in less than four minutes.

THE TEXAS BABE

She never said she was good. She just said she was trying to get better. But she knew how to take a dare.

Mildred was 17 and played outfield for the Dallas Dudes. She could run and catch with the best of them. But most of all she could throw.

Many times a runner with a good hit would round first and try for second. He would think he had a two-base hit. But if Mildred got the ball, he was lost. It would fly from her hand straight to the second baseman.

It was summertime. The Dudes were starting their day's work. They were getting ready for their next game.

Mildred started throwing to the catcher to warm up her arm. She threw fast and hard, the way she did in her own back yard.

The coach, standing near the catcher, saw her. "Don't knock the man down, kid," he joked.

"I'm used to throwing that way," Mildred answered.

The coach laughed. Maybe some day, he said, she could break the record for a baseball throw.

Mildred walked over to him. "O.K.. What's the record? Now's as good a time as any."

The coach smiled at the catcher. Then he told Mildred, "I'll trot out there 295 feet. Send it to me from home, kid."

As the coach walked out into the field, he counted each step. When he thought he was 295 feet away, he stopped and turned.

The coach put his hand up above his eyes. So did the other men. They all stopped throwing and stood still on the grass.

It was so quiet that Mildred's ears rang. A fly buzzed by her cap. In back of the stands, someone was whistling. Far away, cars honked.

Mildred caught the ball the catcher threw her. Then she walked over to home plate. There she turned to face the field.

It was the biggest piece of green grass in the world. Was she going to look silly? She never said she was good. She just said she was trying to get better.

Mildred planted her feet. She pulled her arm back and around once—again—and let go. Heads turned as the ball sailed out over the big, green field.

The coach didn't move. The ball kept coming. It was high and small. Then it was over his head. He turned quickly. The ball had come down just behind him!

All the Dudes kept still at first. Then they shouted and ran over to home plate. It was a great throw, a *great* throw, they told Mildred.

But the coach stayed where he was, shaking his head. He was smiling, but not the same way he had smiled at the catcher. This smile was bigger.

The coach couldn't know, that day in 1929, that Mildred was just getting started. For Mildred was Babe Didrikson—later Babe Didrikson Zaharias.

She became one of the greatest women in sports. She broke more records than she could count—in jumping, running, basketball, golf, and many other sports.

Maybe she laughed a little to herself whenever she broke a new record. Maybe the Texas Babe was thinking of the dare she took in Dallas, where it all started.

TIME OUT AT THE OLYMPICS

At first the newspapers made fun of him. But the Reverend Robert E. Richards kept at it. By 1952 he was one of the world's best pole vaulters.

Bob Richards had been in the Olympics before and placed third. Now he was ready for another try.

That is, all of him was ready but his left leg. Bob had hurt his leg a short time before. And it was the leg he needed to push off with.

His leg might hold up for the Olympics and it might not. He had to try. Four more years until the next Olympics was too long to wait.

At the Olympics, Bob made it over the bar again and again. He was scared. But his leg held up. One after another, the other jumpers dropped out. At last only Bob and one other man were left.

The bar was put at 14 feet 9 inches. Both men made it over. Then, as 70,000 people looked on, the bar was put at 14 feet 11 inches.

Each man would get three tries.

On the first two tries, both men missed! On the last try, the other man made it over. But he hit the bar on his way down.

Now it was Bob's turn—his last turn. The wind wasn't blowing the right way. And he had been jumping for six hours now. How much longer could his leg hold?

Bob was about ready to start when, all at once, he put his pole on the ground. He stood very still, with his head down. The people were quiet with him, waiting.

Then Bob Richards started his run. As he came close to the bar, he felt that something wasn't right. His run was off. Just in time, he stopped.

He turned, walked back to the starting point, and started out again.

This time he knew that his bad leg would give him all the push he needed. Up, up, and OVER! He had won the Olympic pole vault and set a new record doing it!

Some people wondered if it had anything to do with that short time he stood still, with his head down.

20 MILES OF WATER

At 7:00 one morning, the young girl walked out into the water and started swimming. The water was still. This looked like a great day for a swim.

Gertrude Ederle was a long way from New York, her home. She was just off France. In front of her, across some 20 miles of black water, was England.

A large boat kept even with her as she swam. It carried her father, her sister, and her helpers.

Trudy had tried this swim the year before, when she was 18, but failed. Her helpers had pulled her out of the water after eight hours; she was crying.

Many others had tried and given up. Only five people had ever made it across. And all five of them were men!

But Trudy had spent a year getting ready for this swim. She wanted so much to be the first woman to swim the English Channel.

One of the men in the boat called to her to slow down. He told her she was starting out too fast. "I'm fine," she shouted back.

As she swam, she began singing about New York. "East side, west side, all around the town. . . ."

Her father had told her he would give her a car if she made it. He kept telling her about it.

Hours passed. The captain thought she had already been in the water too long. He wanted her to come out. But there was that car. . . .

As the day grew longer, the wind changed. It looked like rain. The wind blew harder and harder. The waves got higher. They hit Trudy's head hard as she swam. She began to feel sick, but she kept going.

Night, storm, and black waves. The men in the boat were afraid for Trudy.

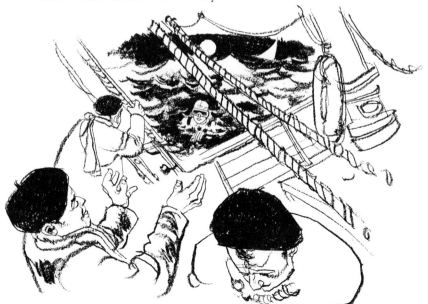

The captain was very afraid. He knew what swimming the Channel was like; he had been one of the five men who had done it. He knew what Trudy must be going through.

England wasn't far now. But Trudy had been in the water for 11 hours! One leg wasn't kicking right any more. She couldn't last much longer, the captain thought.

He had one of the men call to her, above the wind, "Trudy! You must come out!"

"What for?" Trudy shouted back. That car, a red one....

The rain kept falling. It was like a gray wall. Someone on the boat started singing "The Star-Spangled Banner," Trudy joined in.

In England, people waiting near the water heard that the young girl was still swimming. They all turned on the lights of their cars. Trudy's helpers could see the lights as their boat rolled, riding the great waves.

Now, above the wind and the rain, Trudy heard a new sound. It was the sound of car horns! The people waiting for her were all sounding their horns together. They were telling Trudy that they were with her.

The sound of the horns did something wonderful for the young girl in the water. Tired and cold, she kept swimming. She even swam faster.

When Trudy walked out of the water that night in August, 1926, she walked slowly. She held her head high and her back straight. She had been swimming for 14½ hours.

Her father said he was never sure she would make it across. But Trudy said, "I just knew if it could be done, it had to be done. I did it. And now that I have done it, nothing else matters."

At last a woman had made it across. And she, a 19-year-old girl, had crossed the Channel two hours faster than any man!

But the waves did their work. Trudy would never again hear as well as most people.

But, always, in her mind, she would hear one sound they had never heard. It was the sound of many car horns, calling just to her through the rain.

41

HOGAN AT THE 18th HOLE

Once the newspapers called him a wonder. But now he was just another golfer. His leg hurt a little as he walked across the grass. He was tired.

The people stood where they could see his face. When Ben Hogan's car crashed a year before, they all said it was the end for him. They didn't think he could ever play golf again. But he knew that somehow he had to.

And now he was on his way back to big time golf. This was the fourth day of play. Sam Snead, one of the best men in the country, was in the lead.

As Ben got ready to play the 18th hole, the word went around. Sam had already finished. He had played four rounds in 280 strokes.

Ben was behind, and now he only had one hole left to play. The best he could do would be to tie with Sam. But even to do that, he would have to use no more than three strokes.

Ben knew it could be done. He wasn't that far from the hole. And the people knew it could be done. In the old days, they said, it would have been easy for Ben.

But they could all see his face. They could see how long ago the old days were for Ben. This Ben Hogan looked tired, hurting, lucky just to be alive.

Three strokes to tie. Ben picked some grass and threw it up in the air. He saw it blow a little to the left as it fell. Now he knew what the wind would do to the ball.

If he wanted the ball to go straight, he would have to hit it a little to the right. The wind would pull it back to the left.

This was it. The people were very quiet. Ben knew that if he wanted to make his way back up, he would have to start now. He would have to tie Sam Snead. Three strokes to tie.

He swung. Up—up—up went the ball. Then the wind caught it.

Ben was right about the wind; it did pull the ball. The ball went straight, but it didn't get onto the green. It fell short. Ben wasn't that strong yet.

But he knew he still hadn't lost. He could try to land the ball close to the hole on his next shot. Then he could get it on his third shot.

Again the people grew quiet. Ben walked toward the ball. He hoped he could hit it high enough so it wouldn't roll too far. He didn't want it to roll past the hole.

Ben tried out his swing, then stepped up to the ball. The only sound was wind, blowing through the trees.

Ben swung back and then into the ball. It sailed up over the green. When it landed, it rolled just a little. It stopped about a foot from the hole.

Ben walked over to it. He tried the wind once more, then hit the ball lightly.

Ben was smiling from ear to ear as the ball dropped into the 18th hole.

Newspapermen ran to call in the story. Many people came over to tell Ben how happy they were for him.

Ben went on to win game after game, just like the old Ben Hogan. But the game he thought about most was the one he tied that day in 1950 at the 18th hole. If he had lost, he might *really* be just another golfer.

45

BOOKS IN THE
INTERESTING READING SERIES

123456 ♦ 737271706968